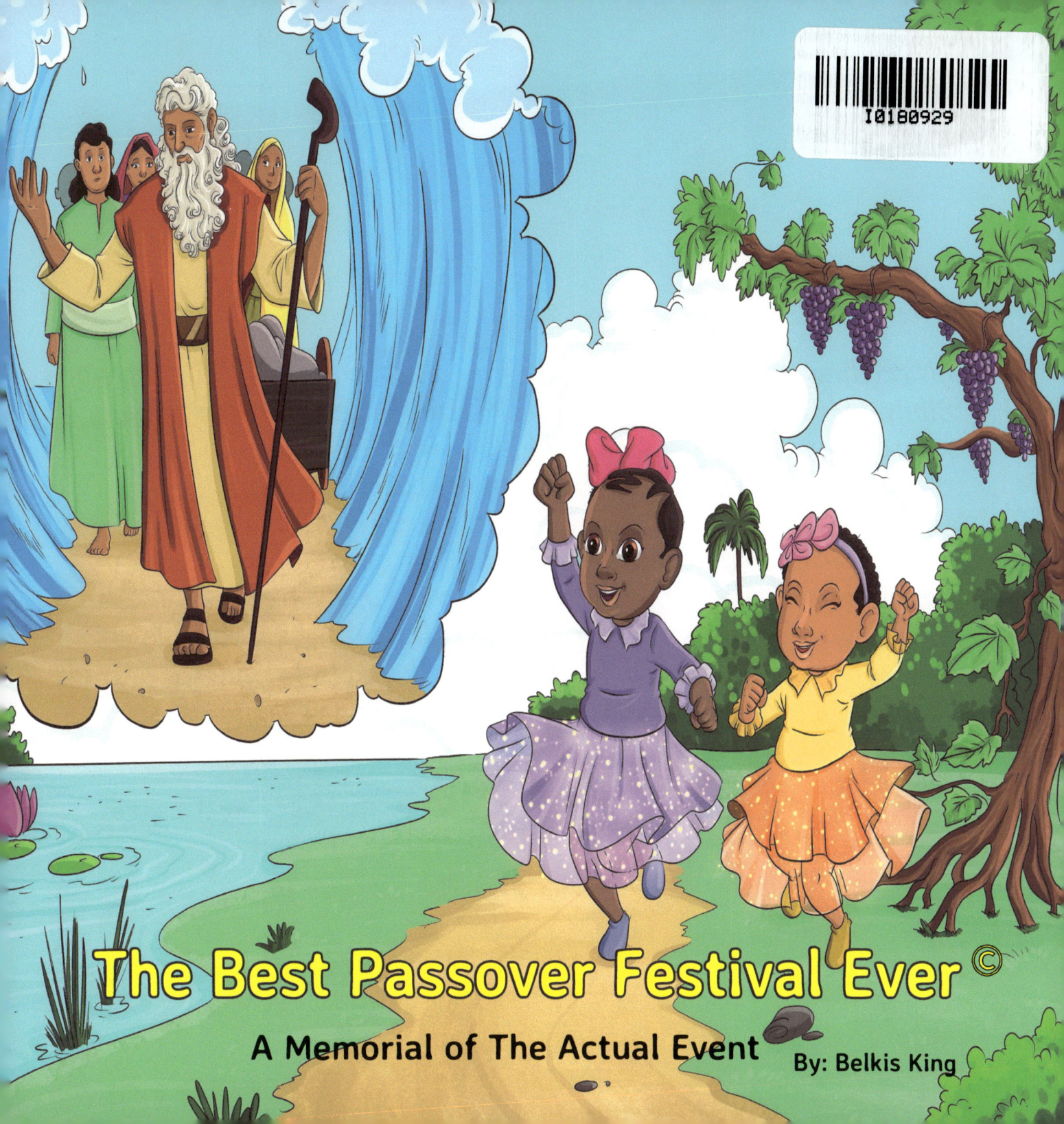

This exciting series of children books contains the ancient ordinances of Biblical festivals, based on historical documented facts from primary sources, first given from God to Moses over three thousand years ago, and later kept by Christ in the New Testament.

Living in such a multicultural world learning about others in the world around us is imperative. I'm inspired to write this book because of our children's love for books and our family's culture. Wishing you all perfect peace within your heart, abundance of overflowing love, and to enjoy all priceless gifts in life. Thank you for purchasing our book series, enjoy!

It's the month of Abib, the first month of the Biblical calendar. Big sister Bayla and little sister Nava are excited because the Passover festival is near!

First, Bayla and Nava diligently help their parents prepare for the festival by cleaning all the leaven out of their house!

Next, they celebrate the festival at Beyth-'el Temple, when the sun begin to go down on Abib 14th. It's a memorial of the exodus from Egypt.

During dinner time, everyone eats roasted lamb, unleavened bread, bitter herbs, takes communion, and washes each other's feet!

Everyone claps, sings, and praises the Lord all night until the morning!

Bayla and Nava invite their friends from all around the world to celebrate the Lord's Passover festival together! Everyone receives special benefits for celebrating the feast according to all of it's ordinances!

Vocabulary words:

Memorial - Something given to remind people that a thing must be remembered forever

Ordinance - Rules or Laws

Citizens - A group of people that belong to the same nation that share the same benefits or commonwealth

1. When does the Passover Festival begin?
2. How many days total is the Festival?
3. Which food ingredients must be cleaned out of the house before the Festival?
4. What are the required foods that must be eaten during the meal on the first night of the Festival?
5. TRUE or FALSE: The first night of the Festival everyone stayed in the Temple until sunrise?
6. Name at least one promise from God for celebrating his memorial Festival?
7. TRUE or FALSE: Communion must be taken only the first night of the Festival?
8. Where must the Festival be kept?

Answers

1. The first month (Abib) 14th day.
2. Seven days
3. Yeast
4. Roasted lamb, bitter herbs, and unleavened bread
5. TRUE
6. Total complete protection, eternal life, and all blessings
7. TRUE
8. Beyth-'el Temple

About the author

Belkis King Shelton was born in the Caribbean Islands of Trinidad & Tobago and moved to the United States as a child with her family being the youngest of six. She has developed her roots in Tennessee were she attended Volunteer State earning a degree in History and Foreign Language. Currently, as a stay-at-home wife of six years with two toddler daughters, over 10 years of volunteering with various organizations in her community, Mrs. King Shelton is a Parent Leader for the state of Tennessee. She also attends Beyth-'el Temple & College under the administration of Dr. Yehohanan B. Amen where she created the series Biblical Festival Children's Books which are translated in several different languages for children across the world to enjoy. Along with her husband, Ben Shelton, and daughters, Bayla and Nava, thank you richly for purchasing the series Biblical Festivals Children's Books.

Biblical References for each Page

Page 1 Ezekiel 45:21

"In the **first month**, in the fourteenth day of the month, ye shall have the passover, **a feast of seven days;** unleavened bread shall be eaten."

Luke 22:1

"Now the **Feast** of Unleavened Bread drew near, **which is** called Passover"

Page 2 Deuteronomy 16:4

"And there shall be **no leavened bread** seen with you in all your coast seven days..."

Page 3 Isaiah 2:2

"And it shall come to pass in the last days, that the mountain of the **Lord's house shall be established** in the top of the mountains, and shall be exalted above the hills; and **all nations** shall flow unto it."

Genesis 28:16,19

"He was afraid and said How awesome is this **place** This is none other than the **house of God**; this is the **gate of heaven**. 19 And he called the **name** of that **place Beth-el** ..."

Duet. 16:5-6

"You may **not** sacrifice the passover **within any of your gates**, which the Lord thy God gives you: 6 But at the **place** which the Lord thy God shall choose to place his name in, **there** you shall sacrifice the passover at even, **at the going down of the sun, at the season** that you came forth out of Egypt"

Page 4   Exodus 25:8

"And let them **make me a sanctuary** ; that I may dwell among them ."

Psalm 100:2
"Serve the LORD with **gladness** : come before his presence with **singing** ."

Psalm 81:3
" **Blow the trumpe**t in the new moon, in the time appointed, on our solemn **feast day** "

Page 5   Luke 22:8

"And he sent Peter and John, saying, Go and prepare us the passover, **that we may eat**.

Exodus 12:8
" That same night they are to **eat** the meat roasted over the fire, along with bitter herbs, **and** bread made without yeast."

1 Corinthians 11:26
"For as often as you **eat** this bread, and **drink** this cup, you do proclaim the Lord's death untill he comes."

John 13:8
"No," said Peter, "you shall never **wash my feet** ." Jesus answered, " Unless I wash you, you have no part with me. "

Page 6 Exodus 23:25

"And you shall <u>serve the Lord your God</u> , and **he shall bless** thy <u>bread</u> , and thy <u>water</u> ; **and** I <u>will take sickness away</u> from among you."

Exodus 12:13

"And the blood shall be to you for a token upon the houses where ye are: and when I see the

blood, **I will pass over you** , and the plague shall **not** be upon you to destroy you, when I smite

the land of Egypt."

Ephesians 2:19

Therefore, you are **no longer foreigners and strangers** , but fellow <u>citizens with God's people</u> and also **members** of his household,

A fun exciting easy to read aloud children's book that gives a comprehensive overview to understand the ordinances of the MEMORIAL Passover Festival. Your child will enjoy the simplicity in the text, vibrant illustrations, and Biblical references on each page!

There are at least seven different ways the term "Passover" is used in the Bible. The following are four distinct examples:

1st

(Exodus 12:14)
Passover: A yearly festival as a memorial of God delivering his people out of the land of Egypt.

2nd

(John 1:29)
Passover: A lamb to take away sin as a sacrifice.

3rd

(Ezekiel 45:21; Luke 22:1)
Passover: A seven day festival called The Day of Unleavened Bread.

4th

(Exodus 12:8,14; Luke 22:8)
Passover: A memorial lamb to EAT, that has nothing to do with sin.

Think of events such as Independence Day or anniversaries, a memorial commemorates the initial event.

This book is a MEMORIAL of the original event that took place in the book of Exodus that the entire family can enjoy with children over and over again!

www.ingramcontent.com/pod-product-compliance
Lightning Source LLC
LaVergne TN
LVHW072117070426
835510LV00002B/91